ZION WILLINGHAM

The Good Shepherd

Are You Called To Pastor?

First edition

This book was professionally typeset on Reedsy.
Find out more at reedsy.com

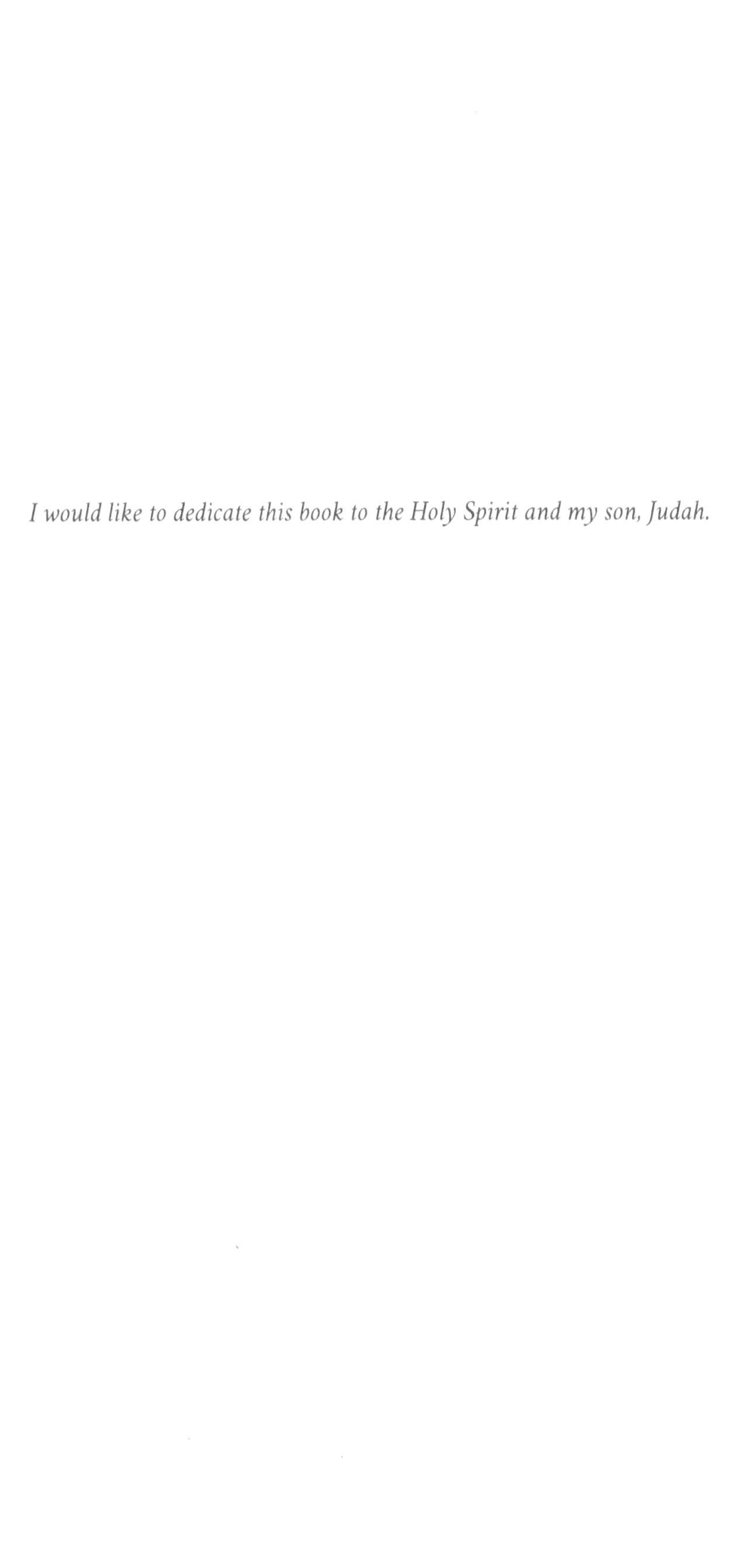

I would like to dedicate this book to the Holy Spirit and my son, Judah.

Contents

Preface

The word pastor is derived from a Latin word meaning shepherd. The word shepherd means to move something from one place to another. The shepherd guides the sheep with love and attention. The pastor can wear all five-fold hats. Are you called to lead and guide? I hope you are. Pastors have been used by God to save and deliver souls from the hands of Satan.

We will discuss the five-fold mandate of the pastor. We will also review its execution in modern times. Come join Zion Willingham as she reviews the call of the pastor, the Good Shepherd.

I

Part One

*The Devil wants you unhappy. He wants you overeating. He
wants you unhealthy. He wants you passive of brain. He wants
you to have nothing distinctive to call your own. He wants you to
have nothing that makes you unique. The devil is a liar.*
-Pastor Bob Hall

1

Introduction

All shepherds are leaders but not all leaders are shepherds. The difference between a shepherd and a leader is that a shepherd walks with the sheep. They lead the sheep. They know the sheep. They develop the sheep. They lead in the midst of the sheep. Jesus gave a very pointed illustration of the job of the shepherd.

John 10:11-13

I am the good shepherd: the good shepherd giveth his life for the sheep.

But he that is an hireling, and not the shepherd, whose own the sheep are not, seeth the wolf coming, and leaveth the sheep, and fleeth: and the wolf catcheth them, and scattereth the sheep.

The hireling fleeth, because he is an hireling, and careth not for the sheep.

The difference between the hireling and the shepherd is three a.m. calls from saints, working and ministering to wounded souls, praying for the saints while others sleep, and genuinely watching for souls.

The shepherd handles ministry in-fighting and church hurts with wisdom and grace. They do this because they are anointed to do this. God installs the grace on those that he calls.

Moses was the first real pastor noted in the Bible. His love for his sheep was so deep that his father-in-law Jethro had to advise him to delegate. (Exodus 18:1-27) He was so much in love with his people that he proclaimed to God that he should have his name removed from the Book of Life for his people. (Exodus 32:32) He so loved the sheep that when Miriam and Aaron spoke against his marriage, Moses was the first person to passionately petition God for mercy. (Numbers 12:13) He had to raise people to carry on while he was on the mountain in prayer, although some of the people still went astray. (Exodus 32:31) He heard from God and was the literal oracle of God. (Numbers 12:7-8)

This is the heart of the pastoral calling. At its core, the pastor is a parent. The definition of a parent is:

": a person who begets or brings forth offspring especially: the natural parents of a child born of their marriage.

To this end, the pastor would be someone who brings forth spiritual offspring.

The definition of a pastor (abbreviated as "Pr" or "Ptr" {singular}, or "Ps" {plural}), is the leader of a Christian congregation who also gives advice and counsel to people from the community or congregation.

Much like a parent advises their children, a pastor advises their flock. A true pastor is vested in the success of the sheep while holding jurisdictional responsibility for all of the saints assigned to their territory.

We will discuss this prestigious calling in greater detail in future chapters.

2

What This Book Is Not

This book is not an instruction manual. It is also not meant to be construed as a call. God is the one who calls. If you are called, God will tell you first. I strongly suggest you review your calling with leadership if you are in a church ministry. If you are not, I urge you to review the resource section to get the training and/or support to assist you with walking in your calling. I do not subscribe to the opinion that all pastors need to go to a school of theology. I do believe that a system of mentorship and training is pivotal to the life of the pastor.

This book is also not a curriculum for the call to pastor. This is an exploration and research book to explore the calling biblically with some slight discussion of the gift in modern times.

If you are called to pastor in any capacity, my prayer is that you will make it your life's priority to manifest. The entire body of Christ is counting on you.

Matthew 9:35-38

And Jesus went about all the cities and villages, teaching in their synagogues, and preaching the gospel of the kingdom, and healing every sickness and every disease among the people.

But when he saw the multitudes, he was moved with compassion on them, because they fainted, and were scattered abroad, as sheep having no shepherd.

Then saith he unto his disciples, The harvest truly is plenteous, but the labourers are few; Pray ye , therefore, the Lord of the harvest, that he will send forth labourers into his harvest.

Simply put, the reason you are a born leader, a natural problem-solver, an excellent listener, and a person who automatically nurtures and develops the gifts in others, is that you are called to pastor. Your innate ability to speak to the needs of people was endowed upon you by God when you were called to pastor. The Kingdom of Darkness sees you as if you are walking in your calling, even if you are not. This is why some people seem to have high-level warfare without operating in a high-level calling. Therefore you would be best served to manifest and position yourself properly.

Whether you are a pastor who oversees a flock in a church or other format. Whether you are a pastor who operates in the marketplace or runs a helps ministry, I pray that this book will fuel a pang of hunger in your soul to manifest. May I pray for you?

May you receive the support and assistance that you need to undergird you in this important calling.

May you bring words of healing and deliverance directly from the throne room of God.

May your character remain strong and stable without controversy.

May your level of anointing and grace continually increase, and may God grace you with the ability to relay wisdom, knowledge, and understanding with skill and the anointing of the Holy Spirit.

May your light extend into the entirety of the location ordained for you, so that you will be a lighthouse for those drowning in darkness.

In Jesus' name, I pray. Amen.

3

Are You A Pastor?

Charles Surgeon said, "Now comes the third question, with which we are to finish. What is that Necessity which is laid upon us to preach the Gospel?

First, a very great part of that necessity springs from the call itself. If a man be truly called of God to the ministry, I will defy him to withhold himself from it. A man who has really within him the inspiration of the holy ghost calling him to preach cannot help it. He must preach. As fire within the bones, so will that influence be until it blazes forth. Friends may check him, foes criticise him, despisers sneer at him, the man is indomitable; he must preach if he has the call of heaven. All earth might forsake him, but he would preach to the barren mountain-tops. If he has the call of heaven, if he has no congregation, he would preach to the rippling waterfalls, and let the brooks hear his voice. He could not be silent." (Spurgeon.org, 2021)

Pastors are often noted as preachers whether actively preaching or not. Why? I believe that Spurgeon hit the nail on the head when he said that when a person receives the call to preach, he must preach. No matter where you put him, he will preach. This overwhelming call can cause discontent for pastors who try to choose other vocations.

What is the thing that you would do, even if persecuted? What is the thing that you would not hesitate to wake up early and stay up late to do? Many of the generals reportedly neglected sleep in favor of grueling work schedules.

I read an article in which the writer quoted lack of meaningful friendships as a sign that you are not called. I disagree. Pastors must be stable enough to be a friend to many people while having very few people that they confide in as friends. I mean that a pastor can sit and listen to the deeply personal problems of their congregation yet they will have very few, if any, members of their congregation with whom they can or even should share their innermost secrets. Pastors have to be in the middle of the herd to be a shepherd, while aloof enough to retain their position in the eyes of the sheep, the wolves, and even the porter. If the sheep no longer respect the shepherd they won't answer his call. (John 10:3-42)

Christianity Today lists great character traits of pastors.

Pastors care for, nurture, and protect others; they value hospitality and time with people. They're great listeners. The pastor in the church is not limited to the pastor of the church. There are loads of professions with a pastoral emphasis—counselors, nurses, and the caring professions. Who were the pastoral types in the Bible? The oikos leaders, perhaps: people like Barnabas, who was known as the Son of Encouragement.

A pastor will have a natural charisma. They usually walk in some aspect of several spiritual gifts. They may not immediately be the best orator, yet God can form an elegant minister from any fully-yielded lump of clay.

Let's see this in action

"Please, Lord," Moses replied, "I have never been eloquent, neither in the past nor since You have spoken to Your servant, for I am slow of speech and tongue."

And the LORD said to him, "Who gave man his mouth? Or who makes the mute or the deaf, the sighted or the blind? Is it not I, the LORD? Now go! I will help you as you speak, and I will teach you what to say."

But Moses replied, "Please, Lord, send someone else."

God was not in the least worried about Moses' speech impediment. He even indirectly took the blame for Moses' speech issues.

Pastors will have received a call to ministry through any means. It may be a dream, vision, or witness of an elder in the church. Many quizzes are designed to help discern the call. I feel that the responsibility of the pastoral call is too great to simply take a career quiz. Charles Spurgeon said that if you can do anything other than preach, do it.

What the Bible says:

Here is a trustworthy saying: Whoever aspires to be an overseer desires a noble task. **2** Now the overseer is to be above reproach, faithful to his wife, temperate, self-controlled, respectable, hospitable, able to teach, **3** not given to drunkenness, not violent but gentle, not quarrelsome, not a lover of money. **4** He must manage his own family well and see that his children obey him, and he must do so in a manner worthy of full respect. **5** (If anyone does not know how to manage his own family, how can he take care of God's church?) **6** He must not be a recent convert, or he may become conceited and fall under the same judgment as the devil. **7** He must also have a good reputation with outsiders, so that he will not fall into disgrace and into the devil's trap.

There will never be too many pastors. As a matter of fact, I would estimate that hurting people outnumber ministers 1,000 to one. Hurting people don't care if you stutter like Moses, have a temper like Peter, or have a thorn like Paul, they simply want the answer to life's questions. Fortunately, the answer to life's questions is Jesus.

4

Five-fold Quick Guide

Five-fold Ministry

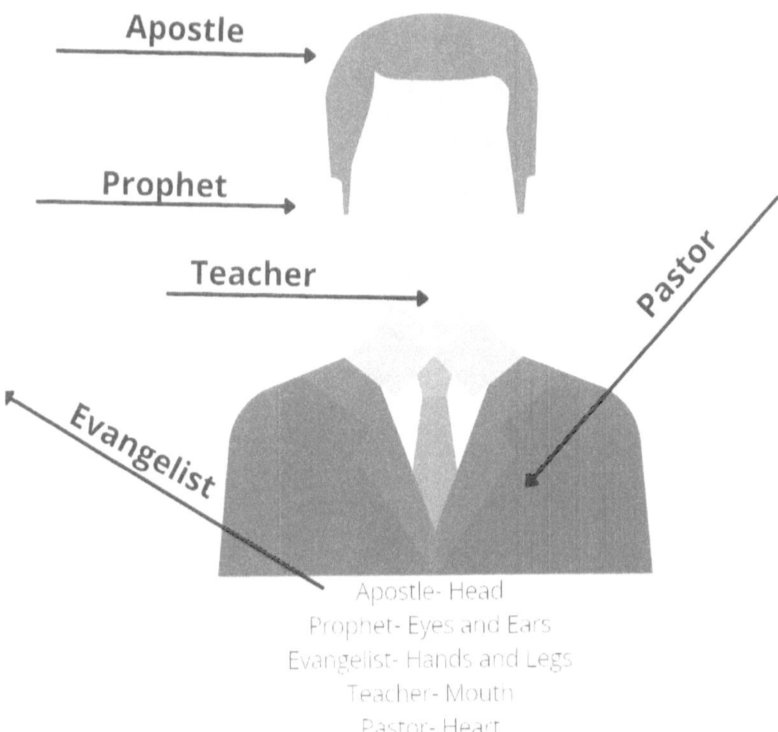

The offices of the five-fold ministry are not titles. There is an erroneous belief that a person is promoted from one level in the five-fold ministry and to another. You will often hear me speak of the apostolic ministry as a high calling. I simply mean that there is a lot of high-level warfare and responsibility.

That notwithstanding, you are not promoted from prophet to apostle. They are two completely different offices.

A good analogy would be:
    Apostle- Doctor
    Prophet- Lawyer
    Evangelist- Politician
    Teacher- Nuclear Physicist
    Pastor- Engineer

Each position has its merit. Unlike positional offices such as bishop and deacon, which can be obtained by an election and are subject to promotion. The work defines the office.

Basic Job Description

Apostle- Build Establish Cover

Prophet- See Hear Relay

Evangelist- Awaken Influence Shift

Teacher- Exhort Interpret Translate

Pastor- Lead Parent Align and Plant

5

Enemies of the Pastoral

Jezebel the Takeover Spirit

Jezebel has a prescribed motive whenever it manifests. A pastor serves a high role in the government of God. This spirit is attracted to this role. To best understand the role of Jezebel in dealing with its hosts, it is best to review the person of Haman in the Book of Esther. This spirit:

1. Appears diligent, hardworking, talented, and loyal.

2. Will stop at nothing to work their way next to the leader.

3. Will find a way to commandeer the authority of the leader and make decisions using the authority of the leader (pastor)

4. Ultimately they want to be the leader. It may take time to manifest, but eventually, they will attempt some sort of a takeover

Let's see this in action

The Deception

Esther 3:8

"And Haman said unto king Ahasuerus, There is a certain people scattered abroad and dispersed among the people in all the provinces of thy kingdom; and their laws are diverse from all people; neither keep they the king's laws: therefore it is not for the king's profit to suffer them."

The commander of authority (through trickery)

Esther 3:10

And the king took his ring from his hand, and gave it unto Haman the son of Hammedatha the Agagite, the Jews' enemy."

Jezebel's real motive

So Haman came in. And the king said unto him, What shall be done unto the man whom the king delighteth to honour? Now Haman thought in his heart, To whom would the king delight to do honour more than to myself?

7 And Haman answered the king, For the man whom the king delighteth to honour,

8 **Let the royal apparel be brought which the king useth to wear, and the horse that the king rideth upon, and the crown royal which is set**

upon his head:

9 And let this apparel and horse be delivered to the hand of one of the king's most noble princes, that they may array the man withal whom the king delighteth to honour, and bring him on horseback through the street of the city, and proclaim before him, Thus shall it be done to the man whom the king delighteth to honour.

The heart of this spirit is always to steal the honor and assume the authority of the leader. Jezebel is often humble and accommodating to leaders while being controlling, manipulative, and vindictive to the people that are beneath it, or that it sees as competition.

Antichrist and Pastoral Burnout

The Bible details that the Spirit of Antichrist will practice "wearing out the saints in the end-times." We are currently in the end-times and the wearing-out campaigns started immediately after the death of Jesus. Let's read more about this.

Daniel 7:25

And he shall speak great words against the most High, and shall wear out the saints of the most High, and think to change times and laws: and they shall be given into his hand until a time and times and the dividing of time.

The argument against this statement is that this scripture is for the time when the Antichrist will appear in political power, not now. My answer is simple.

1 John 2:18

Little children, it is the last time: and as ye have heard that antichrist shall come, even now are there many antichrists; whereby we know that it is the last time.

The Antichrist is an office, much like Satan is an office occupied by Lucifer.

The Kingdom of Darkness has always had someone groomed to step into this role in every generation. Therefore what one antichrist does, another will do because it's a spirit. Therefore if the antichrist will wear out the saints after the rapture, it will wear out the saints before the rapture.

Charles Spurgeon

The Crossway website reports that Charles Spurgeon suffered from severe depression for a good portion of his ministry.

"Aged twenty-two, as pastor of a large church and with twin babies at home to look after, he was preaching to thousands in the Surrey Gardens Music Hall when pranksters yelled "fire," starting a panic to exit the building which killed seven and left twenty-eight severely injured. His mind was never the same again. His wife, Susannah, wrote, "My beloved's anguish was so deep and violent, that reason seemed to totter in her throne, and we sometimes feared that he would never preach again."[1]

Then, from the age of thirty-three, physical pain became a large and constant feature of life for him. He suffered from a burning kidney inflammation called Bright's Disease, as well as gout, rheumatism, and neuritis. The pain was such that it soon kept him from preaching for one-third of the time. Added to that, overwork, stress, and guilt about the stress began to take their toll. And all this was in the public eye and was jumped on by his many critics, not making it easier to bear. The suffering, they argued rather predictably, was a judgment from God."

(crossway.org, 2021)

The natural rigors of maintaining a sincere walk with God and developing others can be hectic. When we factor in demonic arrows it makes the call to pray much more paramount.

The Spirit of Mixed Multitude

Exodus 12:38

And a mixed multitude went up also with them; and flocks, and herds, even very much cattle.

Any ministry inevitably has people within its midst who don't want to know God, grow with God, or act in any genuine way with God. They may have any number of reasons to attend church. Unfortunately, such a person is an open vessel to be used against the church members, the pastor, and the overall church progress

Strife of Tongues

Psalm 31:20

Thou shalt hide them in the secret of thy presence from the pride of man: thou shalt keep them secretly in a pavilion from the strife of tongues

Rumors, accusations, and an endless litany of criticism can be found under the umbrella of the Strife of Tongues.

Witchcraft

In addition, witchcraft has grown to epic proportions. It is a common practice for Western ministers to poopoo witchcraft as the overactive imagination of "less-developed" nations. The truth is that the reason that they are "less-developed" is that they have already been there and done that with witchcraft. Wherever witchcraft propagates, eventually you have slavery, famine, and dispossession of the area. The people are uprooted by God, and the witchcraft spirits simply leech onto the newest society that they can charm their way into.

In her groundbreaking book, He Came To Set the Captives Free, Dr. Brown-Yoder gave the following insights.

"Satan's goal is to make every Christian church like the church of Laodicea described by our Lord Jesus Christ in Revelation 3:15-16: "I know thy works, that thou art neither cold nor hot: I would thou wert cold or hot. So then because thou art lukewarm, and neither cold or hot, I will spue thee out of my mouth." Churches full of passive people who never bother to read or study the Bible, who "Having a form of godliness, but denying the power thereof … " as so well described in II Timothy 3: 5, are not a threat to Satan. We were taught a basic eight-point plan of attack that could be adapted to whatever denomination of church we were sent to.

The fact that most all high ranking satanists regularly attend Christian churches should not be a surprise to anyone. That is, anyone who takes the time to read God's word. We Christians are very clearly warned that Satan's attack will come from within the churches — especially in times of prosperity."

She went on to outline an eight-point infiltration plan that all pastors should keep an eye out for.

1. Profession of Faith (fake)

2. Build Credibility

3. Destroy the Prayer Base

4. Rumors

5. Teach and Change Doctrines

6. Break Up Family Units

7. Stop All Accurate Teaching About Satan

8. Direct Attacks By Witchcraft Against Key Members of the Church (Brown, 1992)

Pastors and their families must be prayed for on a regular basis. It behooves anyone who attends church to pray for the pastor and all of the church leaders

Misplaced Sympathy and the Antichrist

Mark 16:31-23

21 From that time on Jesus began to show His disciples that He must go to Jerusalem and suffer many things at the hands of the elders, chief priests, and scribes, and that He must be killed and on the third day be raised to life.

22 Peter took Him aside and began to rebuke Him. "Far be it from You, Lord!" he said. "This shall never happen to You!"

23 But Jesus turned and said to Peter, "**Get behind Me, Satan! You are a stumbling block to Me. For you do not have in mind the things of God, but the things of men.**"

Jesus recognized this spirit quickly. He could not get around being the most senior member, so he dealt directly with the spirit. This spirit will quietly press a person from their purpose. Whether it's direct through persecution, witchcraft, and mind control, or indirect through playing to character flaws that waylay purpose. This may not always look like a woman quenching a revival. It may look like a trusted aid who purchased alcohol or gambling or helps to arrange illicit affairs for a leader. I have coined the term Misplaced Sympathy, to define this issue. My sincere advice for a pastor or any other minister who seeks to manifest is to;

- Surround yourself with people who love God more than they love you.
- Surround yourself with people who stand to gain more from advancing Christ, than they would gain from association with you.
- If possible try to surround yourself with people who are concerned

with the elevation of the status of the church by their association with you, versus someone who sees your gift as an opportunity to elevate themselves and their cause.

Jesus knew that the antichrist was working to block his ultimate manifestation on the cross. Bless the Lord that Peter's heart was correct. He took the rebuke and learned from it. Some spirits will not go without a violent rebuke.

This theme has continued, whether it is a well-placed "member" of the opposite sex, a spouse immersed in witchcraft, or an enabler at their right hand.

Delilah

I will write much more about Delilah in my book, Delilah. This spirit has been associated with the man-stealing, tight-dress-wearing, bright red lipstick-wearing hussy who comes to church to snatch husbands. Make no mistake, the spirits that possessed Delilah can appear that way when it suits them. The spirits that possessed Delilah always have an agenda. Suffice to say that these spirits stand out in the fact that they truly hate the person that they betray. They will use quiet persistence to gain access to your secrets and then release them to your enemies. Delilah is skilled at hiding until the enemy has arrived. In a church setting, this is the person whom the Devil will use to split the church. I will discuss much more about these spirits in my upcoming book.

I pray that God will give you:

Insight- to be able to see a situation with laser accuracy.

Foresight- to be able to see ahead, with godly vision and discernment.

Hindsight- to be able to look back with divine knowledge and learn from the past, by culling past experiences of themselves and others.

Oversight- The ability to see the full matter clearly.

6

Pastors and Godly Government

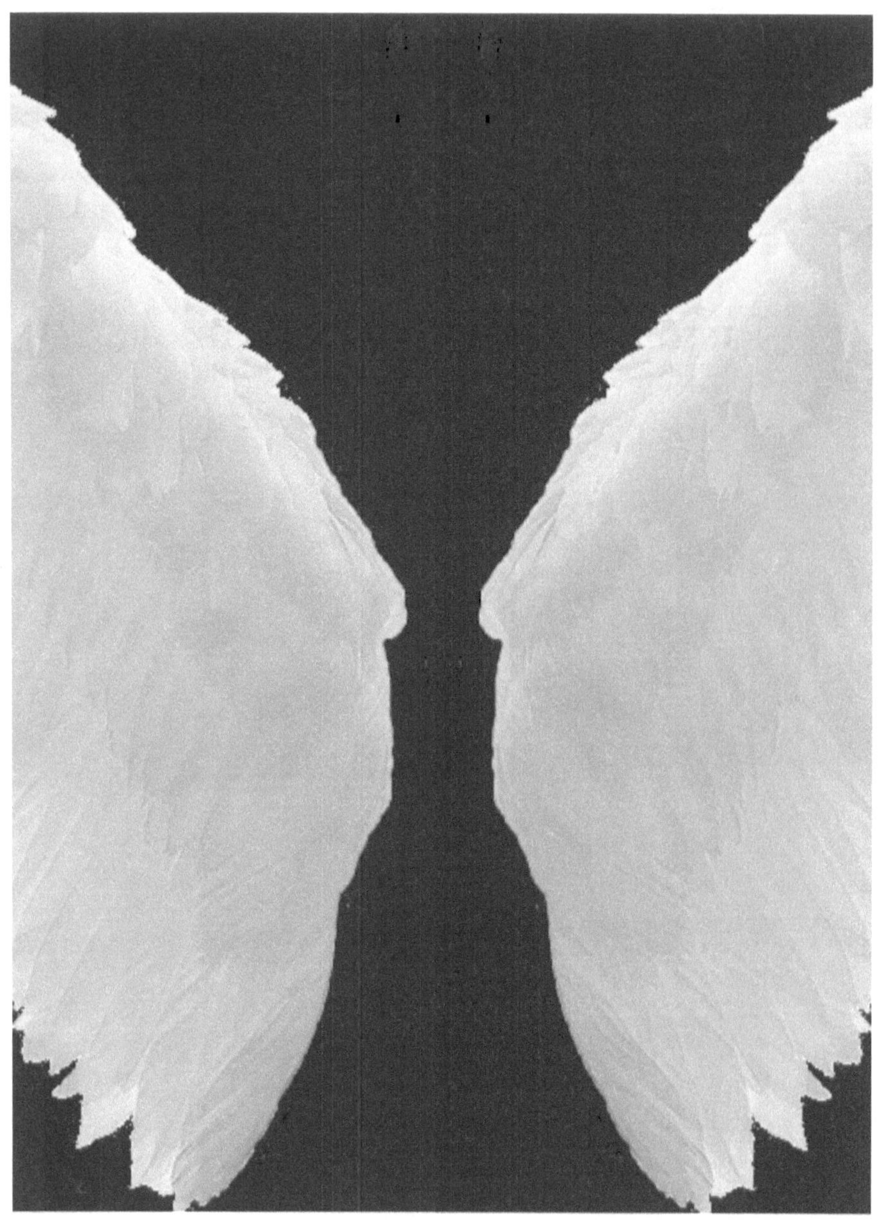

Angels and the Holy Spirit (Taken from Finding The Missing Coin)
The Kingdom of God, or the third heaven, would best be described as

the Kingdom of Light. This light is the driving force behind angels and the movement of the Holy Spirit. The first thing that God did in the first chapter of Genesis was to declare light to exist.

The same was in the beginning with God. All things were made by him, and without him was not anything made that was made.

In him was life, and life was the light of men. And the light shineth in darkness; and the darkness comprehended it not.

There was a man sent from God, whose name was John The same came for a witness, to bear witness of the Light, that all men through him might believe.

He was not that Light but was sent to bear witness of that Light.

The Bible identifies the light. He is identified as the "true light", as opposed to the false light in the Kingdom of Darkness. The Word is the driving force behind the movements of angels and the Holy Spirit. Christians who operate without light are, at the very least, ineffective and fleshly.

Angels are not your servants, no more than your archbishop, general overseer, or apostle is your servant. All of these offices are assigned to minister to the body. It's baffling to see someone who bows down before their human ministry leaders but will refer to angels as their slaves. Angels are sent to minister to each ministry. The word minister means to attend to the needs of someone. Angels are sent to minister to your needs in the same fashion that your Chief Apostle ministers to a local fellowship. He provides oversight and accountability to the leaders. The confusion rests in the fact that it's popular to get in front of people and minister to a congregation by preaching but it's a bit less common to see leaders ministering to the needs beyond the Word of God.

This is not simply financial needs, which some churches address, it's also deliverance ministry, inner healing, personal and professional counseling. Many top-level leaders minister these things to the leaders and pastors under them. This is fine. They may be ministered to by those above them, which is fine. The important thing is that at the top of the human chain is the Angel of the entire ministry. Under that angel is not only the Angel of the overseer but the angels of each ministry. This is the government of God. I will delve deeper into the topic in my upcoming book, The Government of God.

The angels are dignitaries. They take their free will and minister to us compelled by love. Therefore it behooves us to make their work as easy as possible, and stay filled with as much light as possible. Every church has an angel who gives an account for the church. This is why you should never be shocked when angels are spotted during worship services. This is to be expected, as much as it is expected that an archbishop will visit a church they oversee to minister to the people.

The problem lies when no angel covers the church to stand as a lampstand before Jesus. Remember that judgment begins in the house of God. The reason for the angelic absence is usually always an occultist or witchcraft leader. In this case, demons may perform lying signs and wonders through this leader. Two or more praying believers can change such a church, but they need to be led to remain in this church. The Holy Spirit will rarely tell you to remain in a demonic church.

The system of communication with the church is that warnings and exhortations are first communicated to the Angel of the Church, through the Holy Spirit. The Angel of the church will then work with the Holy Spirit to download this message into the spiritual head of that church and assist the leader with its execution. This can be through any method that the Lord sees fit to use.

This process is what it means to be "covered". I have heard a lot of explanations about what a spiritual covering is. It is my understanding that spiritual authority is someone who is so invested in you and your ministry that they are willing to stand before God and man, and give and give an account for your actions. This is the same way a parent would for their children. In Revelation chapters two and three, we hear Jesus directly address the Angels of each of the Churches. This is typical of Jesus. (Matthew 26:40) Jesus addressed Peter about their inability to watch one hour. He went directly to the person who was the highest authority. We hear Jesus say a strange thing in the book of John.

John 17:12

While I was with them in the world, I kept them in thy name: those that thou gavest me I have kept, and none of them is lost, but the son of perdition; that the scripture might be fulfilled.

Jesus was giving an account for his oversight over the church. He was operating in his role as overseer of the early church. He stood as the covering and, therefore, he had to give an account for them.

The government of God is carefully organized. Note that this does not include the home. Christ is the head of the man, and the man is the head of the woman in the home structure designed by God.

Redeemed Christian
    Priestly order of the church
    Angel of the church
    Angel of the Assembly, if large
    Territorial Angels who minister a range from individuals to entire nations

There are angels stationed at every step in the godly government. What a beautiful thing if you establish a fellowship or bible study in your home. House fellowship and even family devotion release light into your home Most importantly the Holy Spirit is here to guide and direct our steps. Hallelujah!

Beyond this, we know that there are seraphim and cherubim because these were mentioned in the Bible. The order of authority of the cherubim and seraphim have been detailed thoroughly by several people of God, through heavenly revelation. We do know that Michael and Gabriel were archangels and that Gabriel stands in the presence of the Lord. I have not read any scriptures indicating which class of angels are above the others. I've heard some really strange things regarding angels. I have even heard someone give the name of the Ninja Turtles and claim that each name is an angelic name!

God has given me no such revelation, and it is not outlined in the Bible. Therefore, I am content to operate in the realm of information that I have personally learned through scripture and experience. God is not in the business of giving us information for only knowledge's sake. Quite the contrary. You may recall that when Jacob asked the name of the Angel of the Lord, the Angel of the Lord immediately asked Jacob why he wanted to know this information. (Genesis 32:29-30).

We learn from the Garden of Eden, the danger of seeking knowledge outside of our rank and capacity. This is for many reasons, one reason is the fact that light also means enlightenment. Lucifer was created to carry light and continues to use the information to capture mankind. Information given at the right time to the right person can change the world. Information given incorrectly can cause destruction. Simply put, there are some things you don't need to know. Technology continues to feed more information into Satan's systems, and he continues to use technology to pump serpentine knowledge out of his systems. The more wisdom a man receives from dark light, the weaker and more evil he becomes.

Elohim is the Father, the Son, and the Holy Spirit, and as one is the head of the Government of God. Several scriptures explain how we should interact with the Government of God. The Bible says to obey those who have the rule over you for they watch for your soul. (Hebrews 13:17) The word "for' in this sentence is qualified by the word watch. If can be replaced with the word "because" for clarity. Many people have misquoted this scripture to mean their local or national government. There are several reasons why this cannot be correct.

By virtue of who they are, the human government is not watching for your soul. How could a person in human government be watching for your soul? They are not allowed to esteem one religion above another, in the course of their business. This fact alone disqualifies the human government as the subject of this scripture. Remember the government and the religious establishment of those times were hostile to Christianity. They repeatedly ordered the Apostles to stop preaching the Gospel, yet all of the apostles continued to preach regardless of what was spoken by the religious and human governmental establishment

Hebrews 13:17

God used the term grieve. A person in human governmental authority is not grieved by a Christian. This would have been someone whose job it is to protect you. This is a more personal relationship. It's a relationship that you can choose to continually ignore or pervert their counsel, like a parent. Ask any Pastor of a local assembly. The entire congregation may hold them in high esteem, yet flesh issues such as in-fighting and personalities can certainly grieve a leader.

On the other hand, there are times when the two intersect, such as Cyrus, who was prophesied years before his occupation of ancient Babylon. God said he "held Cyrus' hand." (Isaiah 45:1) Cyrus would have intersected into godly government by a relationship with God. Even though he was quite unaware that he even had a relationship with God. In other words, he was prophesied in the scrolls years before he arrived, and his inclusion in this scripture was a relationship between two governments.

Romans 13

Let every soul be subject unto the higher powers. For there is no power but of God: the powers that be are ordained of God.

Whosoever, therefore, resisteth the power, resisteth the ordinance of God: and they that resist shall receive to themselves damnation.

For rulers are not a terror to good works, but evil. Wilt thou then not be afraid of the power? do that which is good, and thou shalt have praise of the same:

For he is the minister of God to thee for good. But if thou do that which is evil, be afraid; for he beareth not the sword in vain: for he is the minister of God, a revenger to execute wrath upon him that doeth evil.

Wherefore ye must need be subject, not only for wrath but also for conscience sake.

For this cause pay ye tribute also: for they are God's ministers, attending continually upon this very thing.

Render therefore to all their dues: a tribute to whom tribute is due; custom to whom custom; fear to whom fear; honour to whom honour.

Now let's read Psalm 149:7-9

To execute vengeance upon the heathen, and punishments upon the people;

To bind their kings with chains, and their nobles with fetters of iron;

To execute upon them the judgment written: this honour have all his saints. Praise ye the Lord.

So it's obvious that he does not mean the Government of man. He meant the Government of God. On the other hand, God did not leave the issue of the Government of Man unaddressed.

1 Timothy 2:2
   (Pray) For kings, and for all (both kingdoms) that are in authority; that we may lead a quiet and peaceable life in all godliness and honesty.

Did you notice the qualifier? Pray for the leaders and government of the world and of God, that they will not become a tool in the hand of the Devil. God is not interested in complaints about the government, he wants us to pray! Every time you pray the Lord's prayer you are accepting responsibility to pray for your environment. "Thy will be done, in the earth, as it is in heaven" means that not only are you praying for the Kingdom to come, but you are also praying for a light environment that will facilitate the will of God in the earth, as it is facilitated in heaven.

Paul was not against the human government. Do you remember Sergius Paulus? This man earnestly desired to learn about Jesus, yet he had a wizard blocking him from coming into the saving knowledge of Jesus Christ. This wizard was Elymas the sorcerer. Paul understood that God intended to save Sergius Paulus and therefore he openly confronted Elymas. The physical manifestation of Elymas' spiritual state was the result. Sergius Paulus was fascinated by Paul's words but it was the demonstration of the raw power of God that convinced Sergius Paulus to become a Christian. What a wonderful testimony! (Acts 13:6-12)

The presence of a covering does not affect your responsibility to maintain an upright walk with God. The fact that you have someone over you, who is watching for your soul, means that you should be more spiritual! Remember you are not to grieve the covering over your head.

You are accountable for your walk, and for praying for anyone assigned to you. It is by the Word that the attacks and blessings are determined over our lives. This is why it pays to be a relentless Word reader. A major deliverance pioneer advised reading the Bible continually, even if you don't understand one hundred percent what you are reading. He stressed the importance of giving the Holy Spirit something to work with. I agree. Read what you do understand, and study what you don't. Studying is a surefire way to memorize scripture. Look up difficult words or read parallel translations. The greater your Word level, the greater the light that you carry. The Word of God operates in two dimensions, which are the letter and the principles of the letter.

The letter is the actual scripture. This includes scripture memorization and exegesis of particular words. It is easier than ever to get the tools to decipher components of the letter that you don't understand. Gone are the days when a Strong's Concordance was a major expense. Now you can have a fully functioning Strong's Concordance, as well as any translation of the Bible, downloaded in minutes for free. It occurred to me that Lucifer may be behind the proliferation of Bibles and other materials. Why would he do this? Simply because all excuses are removed. He can walk in the office of Satan (accuser) easier than ever. This is because it has never been this easy to get the letter. The problem lies not in the availability of the letter. It's the mass amount of information overload heaped on everyone. Therefore you have people experiencing choice paralysis, or overchoice, when it comes to a focused study of the Word of God. Social media, television, and any number of other things create a complete overload and hampers focus. The solution to this is timeless, The solution is the hunger and thirst for righteousness. Hunger and thirst for righteousness will always yield a desire to read the Word of God. A determination to embark on a focused study of the Word is also profitable.

The principles of the letter are what is deposited into you when you receive the Word. The principles of God can be likened to a flashlight that will continue to shine brightly as long as it's turned on. The more you receive and conform to godly principles, the more light you will possess. This is how you walk and live, in the Kingdom of God.

I received a funny analogy of the role of warrior angels. In my younger days, I watched professional wrestling entertainment. So often you would see the good guy win a match, and then the bad guys gang up against him and beat him. Suddenly you will hear theme music as another good guy runs to the ring with a chair or baseball bat to clear the ring. The good guy would immediately regain his strength and the good and bad guy would fight to run away the bad guys. According to the Book of Daniel, this is how it works in the heavenly realm with the angels. Therefore, it's safe to assume that this is how it works with us. (Daniel 10:12-20) Glory to God!

7

Prayers for Pastors

I ask that all current future and loved ones of pastors will anoint their scalp, the back of their head, and both eyes.

<u>Pray this way</u>

Father in the name of Jesus I pray that you will open clear dimensions of sight in Pastor ____________

Let the grace on their life grow triple-fold in the name of Jesus.

May they have continuous interactions with their angelic team in the name of Jesus.

Father, please release strange anointings and grace for miracles, signs, and wonders into his life. In the name of Jesus.

Father buttress their vision with kingdom financiers to fund the mandates you place upon their life.

Cover and protect their lives and that of their families as they travel to do your will.

In Jesus' name, we pray.

8

Resources

Free Training
  Biblical Training

https://www.biblicaltraining.org

Christian Leadership Institute
https://www.christianleadersinstitute.org/get-ordained-online/

Church of Hope
http://www.coh.org.au/downloads

Pastoral Care Training
https://smartfaith.net/training-courses/pastoral-care-training/

Church Fuel
https://churchfuel.com/free/

Training Online
Liberty University
https://www.liberty.edu/online/divinity/bachelors/certificate/christian-ministry/

Helpful Resources
TCM
https://tonycooke.org/articles-by-tony-cooke/pastor-resource-links/

The Pastors Wallet
https://pastorswallet.com/free-resources/

There are a pluthora of paid training options for pastors, therefore I did not list them.

9

Arise To Manifest

Arise to Manifest

Thank you for purchasing the first installment in the arise to Manifest series of booklets. I pray that these books will inspire you to service in the body of Christ. May I pray for you?

Father in the name of Jesus. I pray that this book and all others in this series will create a hunger for the work of God.

May the zeal for your house consume every apostle, prophet, evangelist, teacher, and pastor who reads this booklet.

Oh God, inspire them to be the change that we need to see.

Oh God, reveal to them their purpose in manifesting.

May the works of the devil be destroyed by every reader of these booklets.

In Jesus name, we pray, amen

10

References

https://www.spurgeon.
  , wherein org/resource-library/blog-entries/13-spurgeon-quotes-on-calli
ng/

https://www.thegospelcoalition.org/blogs/kevin-deyoung/a-quibble-with-s
purgeon/

II

Part Two

The Lord is my shepherd; I shall not want.

*He maketh me to lie down in green pastures: he leadeth me beside
the still waters.*

*He restoreth my soul: he leadeth me in the paths of righteousness
for his name's sake.*

*Yea, though I walk through the valley of the shadow of death, I will
fear no evil: for thou art with me; thy rod and thy staff they
comfort me.*

*Thou preparest a table before me in the presence of mine enemies:
thou anointest my head with oil; my cup runneth over.*

*Surely goodness and mercy shall follow me all the days of my life:
and I will dwell in the house of the Lord for ever*

11

Biblical Words for Pastors

Hebrews 6:10 (King James Version)

For God is not unrighteous to forget your work and labour of love, which ye have shewed toward his name, in that ye have ministered to the saints, and do minister

2 Timothy 3:16-17

All scripture is given by inspiration of God, and is profitable for doctrine, for reproof, for correction, for instruction in righteousness: That the man of God may be perfect, thoroughly furnished unto all good works

Isaiah 28:9-11

King James Version

Whom shall he teach knowledge? and whom shall he make to understand doctrine? them that are weaned from the milk, and drawn from the breasts.

For precept must be upon precept, precept upon precept; line upon line, line upon line; here a little, and there a little:

For with stammering lips and another tongue will he speak to this people.

Exodus 18:21

Moreover thou shalt provide out of all the people able men, such as fear God, men of truth, hating covetousness; and place such over them, to be rulers of thousands, and rulers of hundreds, rulers of fifties, and rulers of tens

Judges 8:23

And Gideon said unto them, I will not rule over you, neither shall my son rule over you: the Lord shall rule over you

2 Timothy 3:14-17 ESV

But as for you, continue in what you have learned and have firmly believed, knowing from whom you learned it and how from childhood you have been acquainted with the sacred writings, which are able to make you wise for salvation through faith in Christ Jesus. All Scripture is breathed out by God and profitable for teaching, for reproof, for correction, and for training in righteousness, that the man of God may be competent, equipped for every good work.

Nehemiah 8:8 ESV

They read from the book, from the Law of God, clearly, and they gave the sense, so that the people understood the reading.

Deuteronomy 11:18-19 ESV

"You shall therefore lay up these words of mine in your heart and in your soul, and you shall bind them as a sign on your hand, and they shall be as frontlets between your eyes. You shall teach them to your children, talking of them when you are sitting in your house, and when you are walking by the way, and when you lie down, and when you rise.

1 Samuel 12:23 ESV

Moreover, as for me, far be it from me that I should sin against the Lord by ceasing to pray for you, and I will instruct you in the good and the right way.

Ephesians 5:11-13

And he gave some, apostles; and some, prophets; and some, evangelists; and some, pastors and teachers;

12 For the perfecting of the saints, for the work of the ministry, for the edifying of the body of Christ:

13 Till we all come in the unity of the faith, and of the knowledge of the Son of God, unto a perfect man, unto the measure of the stature of the fulness of Christ

1 Corinthians 3:5-9

5What then is Apollos? And what is Paul? They are servants through whom you believed, as the Lord has assigned to each his role. 6I planted the seed and Apollos watered it, but God made it grow. 7So neither he who plants nor he who waters is anything, but only God, who makes things grow. 8He who plants and he who waters are one in purpose, a and each will be rewarded according to his labor. 9For we are God's fellow workers; you are God's field, God's building.

Ephesians 4:11 ESV

And he gave the apostles, the prophets, the evangelists, the shepherds and teachers,

2 Timothy 4:2 ESV

Preach the word; be ready in season and out of season; reprove, rebuke, and exhort, with complete patience and teaching.

Ephesians 3:16-19 ESV

That according to the riches of his glory he may grant you to be strengthened with power through his Spirit in your inner being, so that Christ may dwell in your hearts through faith—that you, being rooted and grounded in love, may have strength to comprehend with all the saints what is the breadth and length and height and depth, and to know the love of Christ that surpasses knowledge, that you may be filled with all the fullness of God.

Proverbs 11:25 ESV

Whoever brings blessing will be enriched, and one who waters will himself be watered.

Luke 12:12 ESV

For the Holy Spirit will teach you in that very hour what you ought to say."

1 Corinthians 14:26 ESV

What then, brothers? When you come together, each one has a hymn, a lesson, a revelation, a tongue, or an interpretation. Let all things be done for building up.

1 Timothy 1:7-8 ESV

Desiring to be teachers of the law, without understanding either what they are saying or the things about which they make confident assertions. Now we know that the law is good, if one uses it lawfully,

Colossians 1:28 ESV

Him we proclaim, warning everyone and teaching everyone with all wisdom, that we may present everyone mature in Christ.

1 Peter 3:15 ESV

But in your hearts honor Christ the Lord as holy, always being prepared to make a defense to anyone who asks you for a reason for the hope that is in you; yet do it with gentleness and respect,

1 Corinthians 12:29 ESV

Are all apostles? Are all prophets? Are all teachers? Do all work miracles?

1 Corinthians 9:27 ESV

But I discipline my body and keep it under control, lest after preaching to others I myself should be disqualified.

3 John 1:3 ESV / 48

For I rejoiced greatly when the brothers came and testified to your truth, as indeed you are walking in the truth.

1 Thessalonians 1:2 ESV

We give thanks to God always for all of you, constantly mentioning you in our prayers,

1 Chronicles 16:11 ESV

Seek the Lord and his strength; seek his presence continually!

Jeremiah 17:8 ESV

He is like a tree planted by water, that sends out its roots by the stream, and does not fear when heat comes, for its leaves remain green, and is not anxious in the year of drought, for it does not cease to bear fruit."

2 Timothy 3:14-17 ESV

But as for you, continue in what you have learned and have firmly believed, knowing from whom you learned it and how from childhood you have been acquainted with the sacred writings, which are able to make you wise for salvation through faith in Christ Jesus. All Scripture is breathed out by God and profitable for teaching, for reproof, for correction, and for training in righteousness, that the man of God may be competent, equipped for every good work.

Nehemiah 8:8 ESV

They read from the book, from the Law of God, clearly, and they gave the sense, so that the people understood the reading.

Deuteronomy 11:18-19 ESV

"You shall therefore lay up these words of mine in your heart and in your soul, and you shall bind them as a sign on your hand, and they shall be as frontlets between your eyes. You shall teach them to your children, talking of them when you are sitting in your house, and when you are walking by the way, and when you lie down, and when you rise.

1 Samuel 12:23 ESV

Moreover, as for me, far be it from me that I should sin against the Lord by ceasing to pray for you, and I will instruct you in the good and the right way.

12

Wisdom Scriptures

Solomon had the insight to ask for wisdom to lead God's people. The wisest man is the man who takes the time to receive the wisdom of the Lord. I urge every child of God that seeks to manifest to at least read these scriptures.

2 Chronicles 1:10

Give me now wisdom and knowledge, that I may go out and come in before this people: for who can judge this thy people, that is so great?

Wisdom/Chokmah/Chakam

Why Wisdom?

Proverbs 1:2

To know wisdom and instruction; to perceive the words of understanding;

Proverbs 1:3

To receive the instruction of wisdom, justice, and judgment, and equity;

How to be Wise

Proverbs 18:1

Through desire a man, having separated himself, seeketh and intermeddleth with all wisdom

Proverbs 1:7

The fear of the Lord is the beginning of knowledge: but fools despise wisdom and instruction.

Job 28:28

And unto man he said, Behold, the fear of the Lord, that is wisdom; and to depart from evil is understanding.

Psalm 111:10

The fear of the Lord is the beginning of wisdom: a good understanding has all that do his commandments: his praise endureth forever.

Proverbs 8:12

I wisdom dwell with prudence and find out knowledge of witty inventions.

Proverbs 8:14

Counsel is mine, and sound wisdom: I am understanding; I have strength.

Proverbs 9:10

The fear of the Lord is the beginning of wisdom: and the knowledge of the holy is understanding.

Proverbs 1:2

To know wisdom and instruction; to perceive the words of understanding;

Proverbs 1:3

To receive the instruction of wisdom, justice, and judgment, and equity;

Proverbs 1:7

The fear of the Lord is the beginning of knowledge: but fools despise wisdom and instruction.

Proverbs 1:20

Wisdom crieth without; she uttereth her voice in the streets:

Proverbs 2:2

So that thou incline thine ear unto wisdom, and apply thine heart to understanding;

Proverbs 2:6

For the Lord giveth wisdom: out of his mouth cometh knowledge and understanding.

Proverbs 2:7

He lays sound wisdom for the righteous: he is a buckler to them that walk uprightly.

Proverbs 2:10

When wisdom entereth into thine heart, and knowledge is pleasant unto thy soul;

Proverbs 3:13

Happy is the man that findeth wisdom, and the man that getteth understanding.

Proverbs 3:19

The Lord by wisdom hath founded the earth; by understanding hath he established the heavens.

Proverbs 3:21

My son, let not them depart from thine eyes: keep sound wisdom and discretion:

Proverbs 4:5

Get wisdom, get understanding: forget it not; neither decline from the words of my mouth.

Proverbs 4:7

Wisdom is the principal thing; therefore get wisdom: and with all thy getting get understanding.

Proverbs 4:11

I have taught thee in the way of wisdom; I have led thee in the right paths.

Proverbs 7:4

Say unto wisdom, Thou art my sister; and call understanding thy kinswoman:

Proverbs 8:1

Doth not wisdom cry? and understanding put forth her voice?

Proverbs 8:5

O ye simple, understand wisdom: and, ye fools, be ye of an understanding heart.

Proverbs 8:11

For wisdom is better than rubies; and all the things that may be desired are not to be compared to it.

The Character of Godly Wisdom

James 3:17

But the wisdom that is from above is first pure, then peaceable, gentle, and easy to be intreated, full of mercy and good fruits, without partiality, and without hypocrisy.

Proverbs 9:1

Wisdom hath builded her house, she hath hewn out her seven pillars:

Proverbs 15:21

Folly is joy to him that is destitute of wisdom: but a man of understanding walketh uprightly.

Proverbs 15:33

The fear of the Lord is the instruction of wisdom; and before honour is humility.

Proverbs 16:16

How much better is it to get wisdom than gold! and to get understanding rather than to be chosen than silver!

Proverbs 17:16

Wherefore is there a price in the hand of a fool to get wisdom, seeing he hath no heart to it?

Proverbs 17:24

Wisdom is before him that hath understanding; but the eyes of a fool are in the ends of the earth.

Romans 11:33

O the depth of the riches both of In Context and knowledge of God! how unsearchable are his judgments, and his ways past finding out!

Jeremiah 51:15

He hath made the earth by his power, he hath established the world by his wisdom, and hath stretched out the heaven by his understanding.

Job 32:7

I said, Days should speak, and multitude of years should teach wisdom

Job 36:5

Behold, God is mighty, and despiseth not any: he is mighty in strength and wisdom.

Job 38:36

Who hath put wisdom in the inward parts? or who hath given understanding to the heart?

Jeremiah 10:12

He hath made the earth by his power, he hath established the world by his wisdom, and hath stretched out the heavens by his discretion.

Job 11:6

And that he would shew thee the secrets of wisdom, that they are double to that which is! Know therefore that God exacteth of thee less than thine iniquity deserveth.

Job 12:12

With the ancient is wisdom; and in length of days understanding.

Job 12:13

With him is wisdom and strength, he hath counsel and understanding.

Job 12:16

With him is strength and wisdom: the deceived and the deceiver are his.

Isaiah 29:14

Therefore, behold, I will proceed to do a marvellous work among these people, even a marvellous work and a wonder: for the wisdom of their wise men shall perish, and the understanding of their prudent men shall be hid.

Isaiah 33:6

And wisdom and knowledge shall be the stability of thy times, and strength of salvation: the fear of the Lord is his treasure.

1 Corinthians 1:24

But unto them which are called, both Jews and Greeks, Christ the power of God, and the wisdom of God.

Luke 7:35

But wisdom is justified by all her children.

Luke 11:31

The queen of the south shall rise up in judgment?? with the men of this generation, and condemn them: for she came from the utmost parts of the earth to hear the wisdom of Solomon; and, behold, a greater than Solomon is here.

Ecclesiastes 10:10

If the iron be blunt, and he do not whet the edge, then must he put to more strength: but wisdom is profitable to direct.

Proverbs 10:13

In the lips of him that hath understanding wisdom is found: but a rod is for the back of him that is void of understanding.

Proverbs 10:21

The lips of the righteous feed many: but fools die for want of wisdom.

Proverbs 10:23

It is as sport to a fool to do mischief: but a man of understanding hath wisdom.

Proverbs 10:31

The mouth of the just bringeth forth wisdom: but the froward tongue shall be cut out.

Proverbs 11:2

When pride cometh, then cometh shame: but with the lowly is wisdom.

Proverbs 11:12

He that is void of wisdom despiseth his neighbour: but a man of understanding holdeth his peace.

Proverbs 12:8

A man shall be commended according to his wisdom: but he that is of a perverse heart shall be despised.

Proverbs 13:10

Only by pride cometh contention: but with the well advised is wisdom.

Proverbs 14:6

A scorner seeketh wisdom, and findeth it not: but knowledge is easy unto him that understandeth.

Proverbs 14:8

The wisdom of the prudent is to understand his way: but the folly of fools is deceit.

Proverbs 14:33

Wisdom resteth in the heart of him that hath understanding: but that which is in the midst of fools is made known.

Isaiah 10:13

For he saith, By the strength of my hand I have done it, and by my wisdom; for I am prudent: and I have removed the bounds of the people, and have robbed their treasures, and I have put down the inhabitants like a valiant man:

Isaiah 11:2

And the spirit of the Lord shall rest upon him, the spirit of wisdom and understanding, the spirit of counsel and might, the spirit of knowledge and of the fear of the Lord;

The Character of Worldly Wisdom

James 3:15

This wisdom descendeth not from above, but is earthly, sensual, devilish.

Job 4:21

Doth not their excellency which is in them go away? they die, even without wisdom.

Job 32:13

Lest ye should say, We have found out wisdom: God thrusteth him down, not man.

Ecclesiastes 2:21

For there is a man whose labour is in wisdom, and in knowledge, and in equity; yet to a man that hath not laboured therein shall he leave it for his portion. This also is vanity and a great evil.

Ecclesiastes 2:26

For God giveth to a man that is good in his sight wisdom, and knowledge, and joy: but to the sinner he giveth travail, to gather and to heap up, that he may give to him that is good before God. This also is vanity and vexation of spirit.

Job 6:13

Is not my help in me? and is wisdom driven quite from me?

Isaiah 47:10

For thou hast trusted in thy wickedness: thou hast said, None seeth me. Thy wisdom and thy knowledge, it hath perverted thee; and thou hast said in thine heart, I am, and none else beside me.

Jeremiah 8:9

The wise men are ashamed, they are dismayed and taken: lo, they have rejected the word of the Lord; and what wisdom is in them?

Jeremiah 9:23

Thus saith the Lord, Let not the wise man glory in his wisdom, neither let the mighty man glory in his might, let not the rich man glory in his riches:

Jeremiah 49:7

Concerning Edom, thus saith the Lord of hosts; Is wisdom no more in Teman? is counsel perished from the prudent? is their wisdom vanished?

1 Corinthians 1:22

For the Jews require a sign, and the Greeks seek after wisdom:

1 Corinthians 1:19

For it is written, I will destroy the wisdom of the wise, and will bring to nothing the understanding of the prudent.

1 Corinthians 1:20

Where is the wise? where is the scribe? where is the disputer of this world? hath not God made foolish the wisdom of this world?

1 Corinthians 1:21

For after that in the wisdom of God the world by wisdom knew not God, it pleased God by the foolishness of preaching to save them that believe.

Acts 7:10

And delivered him out of all his afflictions, and gave him favour and wisdom in the sight of Pharaoh king of Egypt; and he made him governor over Egypt and all his house.

Acts 7:22

And Moses was learned in all the wisdom of the Egyptians, and was mighty in words and in deeds.

(Satan's Wisdom)

Ezekiel 28:12

Son of man, take up a lamentation upon the king of Tyrus, and say unto him, Thus saith the Lord God; Thou sealest up the sum, full of wisdom, and perfect in beauty.

Ezekiel 28:17

Thine heart was lifted up because of thy beauty, thou hast corrupted thy wisdom by reason of thy brightness: I will cast thee to the ground, I will lay thee before kings, that they may behold thee.

Ezekiel 28:4

With thy wisdom and with thine understanding thou hast gotten thee riches, and hast gotten gold and silver into thy treasures:

Ezekiel 28:5

By thy great wisdom and by thy traffick hast thou increased thy riches, and thine heart is lifted up because of thy riches:

Ezekiel 28:7

Behold, therefore I will bring strangers upon thee, the terrible of the nations: and they shall draw their swords against the beauty of thy wisdom, and they shall defile thy brightness.

Acts of Wisdom

Colossians 1:9

For this cause we also, since the day we heard it, do not cease to pray for you, and to desire that ye might be filled with the knowledge of his will in all wisdom and spiritual understanding;

Colossians 1:28

Whom we preach, warning every man, and teaching every man in all wisdom; that we may present every man perfect in Christ Jesus

Colossians 2:3

In whom are hid all the treasures of wisdom and knowledge.

Colossians 2:23

Which things have indeed a shew of wisdom in will worship, and humility, and neglecting of the body: not in any honour to the satisfying of the flesh.

Colossians 3:16

Let the word of Christ dwell in you richly in all wisdom; teaching and admonishing one another in psalms and hymns and spiritual songs, singing with grace in your hearts to the Lord.

Colossians 4:5

Walk in wisdom toward them that are without, redeeming the time.

James 1:5

If any of you lack wisdom, let him ask of God, that giveth to all men liberally, and upbraideth not; and it shall be given him.

James 3:13

Who is a wise man and endued with knowledge among you? let him shew out of a good conversation his works with meekness of wisdom.

2 Corinthians 1:12

For our rejoicing is this, the testimony of our conscience, that in simplicity and godly sincerity, not with fleshly wisdom, but by the grace of God, we have had our conversation in the world, and more abundantly to you-ward.

Ephesians 1:8

Wherein he hath abounded toward us in all wisdom and prudence;

1 Corinthians 2:1

And I, brethren, when I came to you, came not with excellency of speech or of wisdom, declaring unto you the testimony of God.

1 Corinthians 2:4

And my speech and my preaching was not with enticing words of man's wisdom, but in demonstration of the Spirit and of power:

1 Corinthians 2:5

That your faith should not stand in the wisdom of men, but in the power of God.

1 Corinthians 2:6

Howbeit we speak wisdom among them that are perfect: yet not the wisdom of this world, nor of the princes of this world, that come to nought:

1 Corinthians 2:7

But we speak the wisdom of God in a mystery, even the hidden wisdom, which God ordained before the world unto our glory:

1 Corinthians 2:13

Which things also we speak, not in the words which man's wisdom teacheth, but which the Holy Ghost teacheth; comparing spiritual things with spiritual.

1 Corinthians 3:19

For the wisdom of this world is foolishness with God. For it is written, He taketh the wise in their own craftiness

1 Corinthians 1:30

But of him are ye in Christ Jesus, who of God is made unto us wisdom, and righteousness, and sanctification, and redemption:

1 Corinthians 1:17

For Christ sent me not to baptize, but to preach the gospel: not with wisdom of words, lest the cross of Christ should be made of none effect.

Luke 11:49

Therefore also said the wisdom of God, I will send them prophets and apostles, and some of them they shall slay and persecute:

Luke 21:15

For I will give you a mouth and wisdom, which all your adversaries shall not be able to gainsay nor resist.

Acts 6:3

Wherefore, brethren, look ye out among you seven men of honest report, full of the Holy Ghost and wisdom, whom we may appoint over this business.

Acts 6:10

And they were not able to resist the wisdom and the spirit by which he spake.

The Spirit of Wisdom

Ephesians 1:17

That the God of our Lord Jesus Christ, the Father of glory, may give unto you the spirit of wisdom and revelation in the knowledge of him:

Ephesians 3:10

To the intent that now unto the principalities and powers in heavenly places might be known by the church the manifold wisdom of God,

1 Corinthians 12:8

For to one is given by the Spirit the word of wisdom; to another the word of knowledge by the same Spirit;

Proverbs 1:20

Wisdom crieth without; she uttereth her voice in the streets:

Proverbs 2:2

So that thou incline thine ear unto wisdom, and apply thine heart to understanding;

Proverbs 2:6

For the Lord giveth wisdom: out of his mouth cometh knowledge and understanding.

Proverbs 2:7

He layeth up sound wisdom for the righteous: he is a buckler to them that walk uprightly.

Proverbs 2:10

When wisdom entereth into thine heart, and knowledge is pleasant unto thy soul;

Proverbs 3:13

Happy is the man that findeth wisdom, and the man that getteth understanding.

Proverbs 3:19

The Lord by wisdom hath founded the earth; by understanding hath he established the heavens.

Proverbs 3:21

My son, let not them depart from thine eyes: keep sound wisdom and discretion:

Proverbs 4:5

Get wisdom, get understanding: forget it not; neither decline from the words of my mouth.

Proverbs 4:7

Wisdom is the principal thing; therefore get wisdom: and with all thy getting get understanding.

Proverbs 7:4

Say unto wisdom, Thou art my sister; and call understanding thy kinswoman:

Proverbs 8:1

Doth not wisdom cry? and understanding put forth her voice?

Proverbs 8:5

O ye simple, understand wisdom: and, ye fools, be ye of an understanding heart.

Proverbs 8:11

For wisdom is better than rubies; and all the things that may be desired are not to be compared to it.

Job 15:8

Hast thou heard the secret of God? and dost thou restrain wisdom to thyself?

Job 26:3

How hast thou counselled him that hath no wisdom? and how hast thou plentifully declared the thing as it is?

Job 28:12

But where shall wisdom be found? and where is the place of understanding?

Job 28:18

No mention shall be made of coral, or of pearls: for the price of wisdom is above rubies.

Job 28:20

Whence then cometh wisdom? and where is the place of understanding?

Prophetic Wisdom
Revelation 5:12
Saying with a loud voice, Worthy is the Lamb that was slain to receive power, and riches, and wisdom, and strength, and honour, and glory, and blessing.

Revelation 7:12
Saying, Amen: Blessing, and glory, and wisdom, and thanksgiving, and honour, and power, and might, be unto our God for ever and ever. Amen.

Revelation 13:18
Here is wisdom. Let him that hath understanding count the number of the beast: for it is the number of a man; and his number is Six hundred threescore and six.

Revelation 17:9
And here is the mind which hath wisdom. The seven heads are seven mountains, on which the woman sitteth.

Examples of Wisdom
(Paul)
2 Peter 3:15
And account that the longsuffering of our Lord is salvation; even as our beloved brother Paul also according to the wisdom given unto him hath written unto you;

(Daniel)
Daniel 5:14
I have even heard of thee, that the spirit of the gods is in thee, and that light and understanding and excellent wisdom is found in thee.

Daniel 1:17
As for these four children, God gave them knowledge and skill in all learning

and wisdom: and Daniel had understanding in all visions and dreams.

(Moses)

And thou shalt speak unto all that are wise hearted, whom I have filled with the spirit of wisdom, that they may make Aaron's garments to consecrate him, that he may minister unto me in the priest's office.

Exodus 31:3

And I have filled him with the spirit of God, in wisdom, and in understanding, and in knowledge, and in all manner of workmanship,

Exodus 31:6

And I, behold, I have given with him Aholiab, the son of Ahisamach, of the tribe of Dan: and in the hearts of all that are wise hearted I have put wisdom, that they may make all that I have commanded thee;

Exodus 35:31

And he hath filled him with the spirit of God, in wisdom, in understanding, and in knowledge, and in all manner of workmanship;

Exodus 35:35

Them hath he filled with wisdom of heart, to work all manner of work, of the engraver, and of the cunning workman, and of the embroiderer, in blue, and in purple, in scarlet, and in fine linen, and of the weaver, even of them that do any work, and of those that devise cunning work.

Deuteronomy 4:6

Keep therefore and do them; for this is your wisdom and your understanding in the sight of the nations, which shall hear all these statutes, and say, Surely this great nation is a wise and understanding people.

(Joshua)

Deuteronomy 34:9

And Joshua the son of Nun was full of the spirit of wisdom; for Moses had laid his hands upon him: and the children of Israel hearkened unto him, and did as the Lord commanded Moses.

(Daniel)

Daniel 1:20

And in all matters of wisdom and understanding, that the king enquired of them, he found them ten times better than all the magicians and astrologers that were in all his realm.

Daniel 2:14

Then Daniel answered with counsel and wisdom to Arioch the captain of the king's guard, which was gone forth to slay the wise men of Babylon:

Daniel 2:20

Daniel answered and said, Blessed be the name of God for ever and ever: for wisdom and might are his:

Daniel 2:21

And he changeth the times and the seasons: he removeth kings, and setteth up kings: he giveth wisdom unto the wise, and knowledge to them that know understanding:

Daniel 2:23

I thank thee, and praise thee, O thou God of my fathers, who hast given me wisdom and might, and hast made known unto me now what we desired of thee: for thou hast now made known unto us the king's matter.

Daniel 2:30

But as for me, this secret is not revealed to me for any wisdom that I have more than any living, but for their sakes that shall make known the interpretation to the king, and that thou mightest know the thoughts of thy heart.

Daniel 5:11

There is a man in thy kingdom, in whom is the spirit of the holy gods; and in the days of thy father light and understanding and wisdom, like the wisdom of the gods, was found in him; whom the king Nebuchadnezzar thy father, the king, I say, thy father, made master of the magicians, astrologers, Chaldeans, and soothsayers;

The Wisdom of Jesus

Micah 6:9

The Lord's voice crieth unto the city, and the man of wisdom shall see thy name: hear ye the rod, and who hath appointed it.

Matthew 11:19

The Son of man came eating and drinking, and they say, Behold a man gluttonous, and a winebibber, a friend of publicans and sinners. But wisdom is justified of her children.

Matthew 12:42

The queen of the south shall rise up in the judgment with this generation, and shall condemn it: for she came from the uttermost parts of the earth to hear the wisdom of Solomon; and, behold, a greater than Solomon is here.

Matthew 13:54

And when he was come into his own country, he taught them in their synagogue, insomuch that they were astonished, and said, Whence hath this man this wisdom, and these mighty works?

Mark 6:2

And when the sabbath day was come, he began to teach in the synagogue: and many hearing him were astonished, saying, From whence hath this man these things? and what wisdom is this which is given unto him, that even such mighty works are wrought by his hands?

Luke 1:17

And he shall go before him in the spirit and power of Elias, to turn the hearts of the fathers to the children, and the disobedient to the wisdom of the just; to make ready a people prepared for the Lord.

Luke 2:40

And the child grew, and waxed strong in spirit, filled with wisdom: and the grace of God was upon him.

Luke 2:52

And Jesus increased in wisdom and stature, and in favour with God and man.

Wise Nuggets

Proverbs 18:4

The words of a man's mouth are as deep waters, and the wellspring of wisdom as a flowing brook.

Proverbs 19:8

He that getteth wisdom loveth his own soul: he that keepeth understanding shall find good.

Proverbs 21:30

There is no wisdom nor understanding nor counsel against the Lord.

Proverbs 23:4

Labour not to be rich: cease from thine own wisdom.

Proverbs 23:9

Speak not in the ears of a fool: for he will despise the wisdom of thy words.

Proverbs 23:23

Buy the truth, and sell it not; also wisdom, and instruction, and understanding.

Proverbs 24:3

Through wisdom is an house builded; and by understanding it is established:

Proverbs 24:7

Wisdom is too high for a fool: he openeth not his mouth in the gate.

Proverbs 24:14

So shall the knowledge of wisdom be unto thy soul: when thou hast found it, then there shall be a reward, and thy expectation shall not be cut off.

Proverbs 29:3

Whoso loveth wisdom rejoiceth his father: but he that keepeth company with harlots spendeth his substance.

Family Wisdom

Proverbs 29:15

The rod and reproof give wisdom: but a child left to himself bringeth his mother to shame.

Proverbs 31:26

She openeth her mouth with wisdom; and in her tongue is the law of kindness.

Ecclesiastes 1:13

And I gave my heart to seek and search out by wisdom concerning all things that are done under heaven: this sore travail hath God given to the sons of man to be exercised therewith.

Proverbs 4:11

I have taught thee in the way of wisdom; I have led thee in right paths.

Solomon's Wisdom

Ecclesiastes 1:16

I communed with mine own heart, saying, Lo, I am come to great estate, and have gotten more wisdom than all they that have been before me in Jerusalem: yea, my heart had great experience of wisdom and knowledge.

Ecclesiastes 1:17

And I gave my heart to know wisdom, and to know madness and folly: I perceived that this also is vexation of spirit.

Ecclesiastes 1:18

For in much wisdom is much grief: and he that increaseth knowledge increaseth sorrow.

Ecclesiastes 2:3

I sought in mine heart to give myself unto wine, yet acquainting mine heart with wisdom; and to lay hold on folly, till I might see what was that good for the sons of men, which they should do under the heaven all the days of their life.

Ecclesiastes 2:9

So I was great, and increased more than all that were before me in Jerusalem: also my wisdom remained with me.

Ecclesiastes 2:12

And I turned myself to behold wisdom, and madness, and folly: for what can the man do that cometh after the king? even that which hath been already done.

Ecclesiastes 2:13

Then I saw that wisdom excelleth folly, as far as light excelleth darkness.

Financial Wisdom

Ecclesiastes 7:11

Wisdom is good with an inheritance: and by it there is profit to them that see the sun.

Ecclesiastes 7:12

For wisdom is a defence, and money is a defence: but the excellency of knowledge is, that wisdom giveth life to them that have it.

Ecclesiastes 7:19

Wisdom strengtheneth the wise more than ten mighty men which are in the city.

Ecclesiastes 7:23

All this have I proved by wisdom: I said, I will be wise; but it was far from me.

Ecclesiastes 7:25

I applied mine heart to know, and to search, and to seek out wisdom, and the reason of things, and to know the wickedness of folly, even of foolishness and madness:

Ecclesiastes 8:1

Who is as the wise man? and who knoweth the interpretation of a thing? a man's wisdom maketh his face to shine, and the boldness of his face shall be changed.

Ecclesiastes 8:16

When I applied mine heart to know wisdom, and to see the business that is done upon the earth: (for also there is that neither day nor night seeth sleep with his eyes:)

Ecclesiastes 9:10

Whatsoever thy hand findeth to do, do it with thy might; for there is no work, nor device, nor knowledge, nor wisdom, in the grave, whither thou goest.

Ecclesiastes 9:13

This wisdom have I seen also under the sun, and it seemed great unto me:

Ecclesiastes 9:15

Now there was found in it a poor wise man, and he by his wisdom delivered the city; yet no man remembered that same poor man.

Ecclesiastes 9:16

Then said I, Wisdom is better than strength: nevertheless the poor man's wisdom is despised, and his words are not heard.

Ecclesiastes 9:18

Wisdom is better than weapons of war: but one sinner destroyeth much good.

Ecclesiastes 10:1

Dead flies cause the ointment of the apothecary to send forth a stinking savour: so doth a little folly him that is in reputation for wisdom and honour.

Ecclesiastes 10:3

Yea also, when he that is a fool walketh by the way, his wisdom faileth him, and he saith to every one that he is a fool.

Salvation

There is never a reason to miss the opportunity to extend salvation.

2 Peter 3:9
The Lord is not slack concerning his promise, as some men count slackness; but

The most important act of faith is **salvation**. God does not want you to perish but he wants you to come into the salvation that was prepaid for you by Jesus Christ. Today is the day of salvation.

Pray This Way

Lord Jesus, I confess and repent of my sins. Please save my soul. I receive you as my Lord and Savior. Amen

About the Author

Also by Zion Willingham

Precept Upon Precept

Are you called, chosen, or simply curious? The manifest series of books will explore each five-fold ministry call from biblical times until now. Precept Upon Precept is the fourth title in the Manifest Series of books. We will discuss the evangelistic calling in its operation throughout the years. It's time to arise and manifest!

Beautiful Feet

Are you called, chosen, or simply curious? The manifest series of books will explore each five-fold ministry call from biblical times until now. Beautiful Feet is the third title in the Manifest Series of books. We will discuss the evangelistic calling in its operation throughout the years. It's time to arise and manifest!

Come Out of the Cave

Are you called, chosen, or simply curious? The manifest series of books will explore each five-fold ministry call from biblical times until now. Come Out of the Cave is the second title in the Manifest Series of books. We will discuss the evangelistic calling in its operation throughout the years. It's time to arise and manifest!

God's Spectacle

Are you called, chosen, or simply curious? The manifest series of books will explore each five-fold ministry call from biblical times until now. God's Spectacle is the first title in the Manifest Series of books. We will discuss the evangelistic calling in its operation throughout the years. It's time to arise and manifest!

Night Battle Plan

Praying at night can be the difference between dumbfounding success or crushing defeat in the day. Night battles have turned many nights into a source of dread for countless sufferers. You can take on the Night Battle and win victories for yourself and others.

Not Quite Human

So what are we going to address in this book? We will find out what the Bible says, once and for all, about such controversial issues as aliens, astral realms, and the the authority of man.

Let's stop avoiding people who make claims about these things and search for the truth. I invite you to journey with me, as we explore those things that are not quite human

Self-Deliverance Manual

What do you do when you need freedom and there is no one available to help? What do you do when the amount of satanic concentration against your life is so thick that Pastors dare not help, for fear of the backlash? What do you do when the enemy has separated you from friends and family, and you can't find one person to agree with you? What do you do when your presence brings irritation and attacks to anyone you come into contact with? What do you do when unexplained demonic activities invade your home? The answer is simple, the method may not be. Deliverance is the answer. So what do you do when there is none to deliver? The good news is that Jesus Christ will deliver you.

The Holy Spirit brings about deliverance through yielded human beings. Therefore it stands to reason that if the extension cord is missing, you will need to plug yourself directly into the outlet of power. Will it be easy? It may or may not be easy. Deliverance can be compared to delivering a baby. It may be hard, long, and involve a lot of effort and pain, or it can be quick and easy. Either way, the results are worth the effort.

In his song, Hear the footsteps of Jesus, William J Kirkpatrick asked, Wilt thou be made whole" The question still lingers today. Do you hear Jesus calling you to be made whole?

Mad As Hell

Hell is mad! To complete your victory, you must execute a madness that surpasses the madness of hell. If you are ready to complete your battle plan, you must exercise a greater level of madness than the powers that began the attack.

Zion Willingham explores an innovative new way to soak your home with prayers during sleep, and while you are away during the day. Use ingenuity to guard your home and perfect your victory in battle.

The final title in the Battle Plan Series will complete your battle with acidic renunciations, radical decrees and brutal pronouncements that are designed to be recorded, and played while you sleep. Read the rules of engagement to your environment, and that of your loved ones,

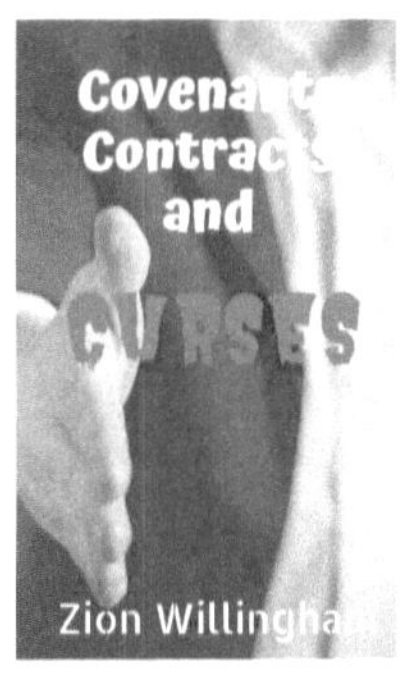

Covenants Contracts and Curses

Every fruit comes from a tree or vine. Every tree or vine comes from a root. Every root started as a seed. In order to chop down a massive tree one must cut down through the root and all seeds must be removed. Curses, Contracts, and Covenants work in the same fashion. This book will help you discern the seed of stubborn oppression, so that you can destroy the tree with its fruit